Sing Ye Merry

Hymns & Carols for Christmas

First Edition

Sing Ye Merry

Hymns & Carols for Christmas

FIRST EDITION

compiled by Joshua M. Jensen

Towner Books

Copyright © 2011 by Joshua M. Jensen. All rights reserved.
ISBN 978-1-105-33224-1

Christmas 2011

for my family, especially RuthAmy, who sings with me

About This Collection

In our home, the Christmas music starts in October, giving us four months to sing and listen to the songs of Christmas (the season, of course, extends into January).

Unfortunately, most hymnals have a rather scanty selection of Christmas carols and hymns, and those included are often missing verses. On the other hand, many books that contain only Christmas music are light on the traditional carols and theologically rich hymns. Hence this book: a collection of texts from many of my favorite Christmas hymns and carols, along with several I would like to learn.

I have taken the texts from the remarkable collection of Christmas songs at www.hymnsandcarolsofchristmas.com. In many cases, there are multiple versions of a song to choose from; I have typically chosen the form most familiar to me. To see all the variants, along with notes, I refer you to the website. Occasionally I have omitted stanzas that I did not like or that I found to be unsingable.

For most texts, I have not included a tune name, on the assumption that the tune is already familiar. In a future edition, I may include more. If there are any songs you think should be included, let me know, and if I agree, I will add your suggestion to the next version. An index of songs included in this book can be found at the back.

My vision for this book is that it will be used by families and friends (specifically my family and friends) to sing *together*: loudly, lustily, and merrily!

Hymns & Carols for Christmas

All my heart this night rejoices

1. All my heart this night rejoices,
   As I hear, Far and near, Sweetest angel voices;
   "Christ is born," their choirs are singing,
   Till the air Everywhere Now with joy is ringing.

2. For it dawns, — the promised morrow
   Of His birth Who the earth Rescues from her sorrow.
   God to wear our form descendeth,
   Of His grace To our race Here His Son He lendeth:

3. Yea, so truly for us careth,
   That His Son All we've done As our offering beareth;
   As our Lamb who, dying for us,
   Bears our load, And to God Doth in peace restore us.

4. Hark! a voice from yonder manger,
   Soft and sweet, Doth entreat, "Flee from woe1 and danger;
   Brethren come, from all doth grieve you
   You are freed, All you need I will surely give you."

5. Come then, let us hasten yonder;
   Here let all, Great and small, Kneel in awe and wonder.
   Love Him who with love is yearning;
   Hail the Star That from far Bright with hope is burning!

6. Ye who pine in weary sadness,
   Weep no more, For the door Now is found of gladness.
   Cling to Him for He will guide you
   Where no cross Pain or loss, Can again betide you.

7. Hither come, ye heavy-hearted;
   Who for sin Deep within, Long and sore have smarted;
   For the poison'd wounds you're feeling
   Help is near, One is here Mighty for their healing!

8. Hither come, ye poor and wretched;
   Know His will Is to fill Every hand outstretched;
   Here are riches without measure,
   Here forget All regret, Fill your hearts with treasure.

9. Blessed Saviour, let me find Thee!
   Keep Thou me Close to Thee, Cast me not behind Thee!
   Life of life, my heart Thou stillest,
   Calm I rest On Thy breast, All this void Thou fillest.

10. Thee, dear Lord, with heed I'll cherish,
    Live to Thee, And with Thee Dying, shall not perish;
    But shall dwell with Thee for ever,
    Far on high In the joy That can alter never.

Paul Gerhardt, 1607-1676
Trans. Catherine Winkworth, 1827-1878

Angels from the realms of glory

1. Angels from the realms of glory,
   Wing your flight over all the earth;
   Ye who sang creation's story
   Now proclaim the Messiah's birth.

   Come and worship, come and worship
   Worship Christ, the newborn King.

2. Shepherds, in the field abiding,
   Watching over your flocks by night,
   God with man is now residing;
   Yonder shines the infant light:

3. Sages, leave your contemplations,
   Brighter visions beam afar;
   Seek the great Desire of nations;
   Ye have seen His natal star.

4. Saints, before the altar bending,
   Watching long in hope and fear;
   Suddenly the Lord, descending,
   In His temple shall appear.

5. Sinners, wrung with true repentance,
   Doomed for guilt to endless pains,
   Justice now revokes the sentence,
   Mercy calls you, break your chains.

6. Though an infant now we view Him,
   He shall fill His Father's throne,
   Gather all nations to Him;
   Every knee shall then bow down:

James Montgomery, 1771-1854

Angels we have heard on high

1 Angels we have heard on high
  Sweetly singing o'er the plains,
  And the mountains in reply
  Echoing their joyous strains.

  Gloria, in excelsis Deo!
  Gloria, in excelsis Deo!

2 Shepherds, why this jubilee?
  Why your joyous strains prolong?
  What the gladsome tidings be
  Which inspire your heavenly song?

3 Come to Bethlehem and see
  Him whose birth the angels sing;
  Come, adore on bended knee,
  Christ the Lord, the newborn King.

4 See Him in a manger laid,
  Whom the choirs of angels praise;
  Mary, Joseph, lend your aid,
  While our hearts in love we raise.

Trad. French carol
Trans. Bishop James Chadwick, 1813-1882

As with gladness, men of old

1. As with gladness, men of old
   Did the guiding star behold
   As with joy they hailed its light
   Leading onward, beaming bright
   So, most glorious Lord, may we
   Evermore be led to Thee.

2. As with joyful steps they sped
   To that lowly manger bed
   There to bend the knee before
   Him Whom heaven and earth adore;
   So may we with willing feet
   Ever seek Thy mercy seat.

3. As they offered gifts most rare
   At that manger rude and bare;
   So may we with holy joy,
   Pure and free from sin's alloy,
   All our costliest treasures bring,
   Christ, to Thee, our heavenly King.

4. Holy Jesus, every day
   Keep us in the narrow way;
   And, when earthly things are past,
   Bring our ransomed souls at last
   Where they need no star to guide,
   Where no clouds Thy glory hide.

5. In the heavenly country bright,
   Need they no created light;
   Thou its light, its joy, its crown,
   Thou its sun which goes not down;
   There forever may we sing
   Alleluias to our King! —*William Chatterton Dix, 1837-1865*

Away in a manger

1. Away in a manger, no crib for His bed,
   The little Lord Jesus laid down His sweet head;
   The stars in the sky looked down where He lay,
   The little Lord Jesus, asleep in the hay.

2. The cattle are lowing, the poor Baby wakes.
   But little Lord Jesus, no crying He makes.
   I love thee, Lord Jesus, look down from the sky.
   And stay by the cradle till morning is nigh.

3. Be near me, Lord Jesus, I ask Thee to stay,
   Close by me forever, and love me, I pray!
   Bless all the dear children in Thy tender care
   And fit us for heaven, to Live with Thee there.

Anon., 1885 (vv. 1 & 2)
John Thomas McFarland, 1851-1913 (v. 3)

The Birthday of a King

1. In the little village of Bethlehem,
   There lay a Child one day;
   And the sky was bright with a holy light
   Over the place where Jesus lay.

   Alleluia! O how the angels sang.
   Alleluia! How it rang!
   And the sky was bright with a holy light
   'Twas the birthday of a King.

2. 'Twas a humble birthplace,
   But O how much God gave to us that day,
   From the manger bed what a path has led,
   What a perfect, holy way.

William Harold Neidlinger, 1863-1924

Break forth, O beauteous heavenly light

1. Break forth, O beauteous heavenly light,
And usher in the morning;
O shepherds, shrink not with afright,
But hear the angel's warning.
This Child, now weak in infancy,
Our confidence and joy shall be,
The power of Satan breaking,
Our peace eternal making.

2. All blessing, thanks and praise to thee,
Lord Jesus Christ, be given;
Thou hast our brother deigned to be,
Our foes in sunder riven.
O grant us through our day of grace
With constant praise to seek Thy face;
Grant us ere long in glory
With praises to adore thee.

Johann Rist, 1607-1677
Trans. John Troutbeck, c. 1885 (v. 1);
Arthur Tozer Russell, 1806-1874 (v. 2)

Bring a torch, Jeanette, Isabella

1. Bring a torch, Jeanette, Isabella
Bring a torch, to the cradle run!
It is Jesus, good folk of the village;
Christ is born and Mary's calling;
Ah! ah! beautiful is the Mother
Ah! ah! beautiful is her Son!

2. It is wrong when the Child is sleeping
It is wrong to talk so loud;
Silence, all, as you gather around.
Lest your noise should waken Jesus.
Hush! hush! see how fast He slumbers!
Hush! hush! see how fast He sleeps!

3. Hasten now, good folk of the village;
Hasten now the Christ Child to see.
You will find Him asleep in the manger;
Quietly come and whisper softly,
Hush! hush! Peacefully now He slumbers.
Hush! hush! Peacefully now He sleeps.

4. Softly to the little stable.
Softly for a moment come;
Look and see how charming is Jesus
How He is white, His cheeks are rosy!
Hush! hush! see how the Child is sleeping;
Hush! hush! see how He smiles in his dreams.

Émile Blémont
Trans. Edward Cuthbert Nunn, 1868-1914

Carol of the bells

Hark! How the bells, sweet silver bells,
all seem to say, throw cares away
Christmas is here, bringing good cheer,
to young and old, meek and the bold,
Oh how they pound, raising the sound,
o'er hill and dale, telling their tale,
Gaily they ring, while people sing
songs of good cheer, Christmas is here,
Merry, merry, merry, merry Christmas,
Merry, merry, merry, merry Christmas,
On on they send, on without end,
their joyful tone to every home
Dong Ding dong ding, dong Bong

Peter J. Wilhousky, 1936
Adapted from "Shchedryk," Mykola D. Leontovych, 1916

Child in the manger[1]

1. Child in the manger, infant of Mary,
Outcast and Stranger, Lord of us all,
Child Who inherits all our transgressions,
All our demerits upon Him fall.

2. Once the most holy Child of salvation
Gently and lowly lived here below.
Now as our glorious mighty Redeemer,
See Him victorious over each foe.

---

[1] Sing to BUNESSAN, tune for "God of the ages."

3 Prophets foretold Him, Infant of wonder;
Angels behold Him on His throne.
Worthy our Savior of all our praises;
Happy forever are His own.

Mary MacDonald, 1789-1872
Trans. Lachlan Macbean, 1853-1931

Come, Thou long-expected Jesus[2]

1 Come, Thou long-expected Jesus,
Born to set Thy people free;
From our fears and sins release us,
Let us find our rest in Thee.

2 Israel's strength and consolation,
Hope of all the earth Thou art;
Dear desire of every nation,
Joy of every longing heart.

3 Born Thy people to deliver,
Born a child, and yet a King,
Born to reign in us for ever,
Now thy gracious kingdom bring.

4 By Thine own eternal Spirit,
Rule in all our hearts alone:
By Thine all-sufficient merit,
Raise us to Thy glorious throne. Amen.

Charles Wesley, 1707-1788

---

[2]Sing to HYFRYDOL or JEFFERSON.

Deck the hall

1. Deck the hall with boughs of holly, Fa la etc.
   'Tis the season to be jolly, Fa la etc.
   Don we now our gay apparel, Fa la etc.
   Troll the ancient Yuletide carol, Fa la etc.

2. See the blazing yule before us, Fa la etc.
   Strike the harp and join the chorus, Fa la etc.
   Follow me in merry measure, Fa la etc.
   While I tell of Christmas treasure, Fa la etc.

3. Fast away the old year passes, Fa la etc.
   Hail the new, ye lads and lasses, Fa la etc.
   Sing we joyous all together, Fa la etc.
   Heedless of the wind and weather, Fa la etc.

Anon.

Ding Dong! merrily on high

1. Ding Dong! merrily on high
   In heav'n the bells are ringing
   Ding, dong! verily the sky
   Is riv'n with angel singing
   Gloria, Hosanna in excelsis

2. E'en so here below, below
   Let steeple bells be swungen
   And i-o, i-o, i-o
   By priest and people be sungen
   Gloria, Hosanna in excelsis

3. Pray ye dutifully prime
   Your matin chime, ye ringers
   May ye beautifully rime
   Your evetime song, ye singers
   Gloria, Hosanna in excelsis.

George Ratcliffe Woodward, 1848-1934

Dives and Lazarus

1 As it fell out upon a day,
  Rich Dives made a feast,
  And he invited all his friends,
  And gentry of the best.

2 Then Lazarus laid him down and down,
  And down at Dives' door;
  Some meat, some drink, brother Dives,
  Bestow upon the poor.

3 Thou'rt none of my brother, Lazarus,
  That lies begging at my door;
  Nor meat nor drink will I give to thee,
  Nor bestow upon the poor.

4 Then Lazarus laid him down and down
  And down at Dives' wall;
  Some meat, some drink, brother Dives,
  Or with hunger starve I shall.

5 Thou'rt none of my brother, Lazarus,
  That lies begging at my wall;
  Nor meat nor drink will I give to thee,
  But with hunger starve you shall.

6 Then Lazarus laid him down and down,
  And down at Dives' gate;
  Some meat, some drink, brother Dives,
  For Jesus Christ his sake.

7 Thou'rt none of my brother, Lazarus,
  That lies begging at my gate;
  Nor meat nor drink will I give to thee,
  For Jesus Christ His sake.

8. Then Dives sent out his merry men,
   To whip poor Lazarus away;
   They had no power to strike a stroke,
   But flung their whips away.

9. Then Dives sent out his hungry dogs,
   To bite him as he lay;
   They had no power to bite at all,
   But licked his sores away.

10. As it fell out upon a day,
    Poor Lazarus sickened and died;
    There came two Angels out of Heaven,
    His soul therein to guide.

11. Rise up, rise up, brother Lazarus,
    And come along with me;
    There's a place in Heaven prepared for thee,
    To sit upon an Angel's knee.

12. As it fell out upon a day,
    Rich Dives sickened and died;
    There came two serpents out of Hell,
    His soul therein to guide.

13. Rise up, rise up, brother Dives,
    And come along with me;
    There's a place in Hell prepared for thee,
    To sit upon a serpent's knee.

14. Then Dives looked with burning eyes,
    And saw poor Lazarus blest;
    One drop of water, Lazarus,
    To quench my flaming thirst!

continued...

15 Oh I had I as many years to abide
     As there are blades of grass,
     Then there would be an end: but now
     Hell's pains will never pass.

16 Oh! were I but alive again,
     For the space of one halt hour,
     I would make my peace and so secure
     That the Devil should have no power!

Trad.

The first Nowell

1 The first Nowell the Angel did say
    Was to certain poor Shepherds in fields as they lay.
    In fields where they lay keeping their sheep,
    In a cold winter's night that was so deep

Nowell, nowell, nowell, nowell.
Born is the King of Israel.

2 They looked up and saw a star
    Shining in the East, beyond them far,
    And to the earth it gave great light,
    And so it continued, both day and night.

3 And by the light of that same Star
    Three Wise Men came from country far,
    To seek for a King was their intent,
    And to follow the Star wherever it went.

4 This Star drew nigh to the North West;
    O'er Bethlehem it took it's rest.
    And there it did both stop and stay,
    Right over the place where Jesus lay.

5 Then did they know assuredly
    Within that house, the King did lie
    One entered in then for to see
    And found the babe in poverty.

6 Then enter'd in those Wise Men three,
    Full reverently upon their knee,
    And offer'd there, in his presence,
    Their gold, and myrrh, and frankincense.

7 Between an ox stall and an ass,
    This Child truly there born he was;
    For want of clothing they did him lay
    All in a manger, among the hay.

8 Then let us all with one accord
    Sing praises to our heavenly Lord;
    That hath made heaven and earth of nought,
    And with his blood mankind hath bought.

9 If we in our time shall do well
    We shall be free from death and Hell
    For God hath prepared for us all
    A resting place in general.

Trad. English carol

Fum, Fum, Fum

1. On this joyful Christmas Day
   Sing fum, fum, fum
   On this joyful Christmas Day
   Sing fum, fum, fum
   For a blessed Babe was born
   Upon this day at the break of morn
   In a manger poor and lowly
   Lay the Son of God most holy
   Fum, Fum, Fum!

2. Thanks to God for holidays
   Sing fum, fum, fum
   Thanks to God for holidays
   Sing fum, fum, fum
   Now we all our voices raise
   And sing a song of grateful praise
   Celebrate in song and story
   All the wonders of His glory
   Fum, fum, fum!

3. Praise we now the Lord above,
   Sing fum, fum, fum.
   Praise we now the Lord above,
   Sing fum, fum, fum.
   For upon this day at morn,
   The wond'rous Son of God was born,
   In a manger poor and lowly
   Lay the Blessed Babe most holy,
   Fum, fum, fum.

Catalan Carol

Gentle Mary laid her Child[3]

1. Gentle Mary laid her Child
   Lowly in a manger;
   There He lay, the undefiled,
   To the world a Stranger:
   Such a Babe in such a place,
   Can He be the Savior?
   Ask the saved of all the race
   Who have found His favor.

2. Angels sang about His birth;
   Wise men sought and found Him;
   Heaven's star shone brightly forth,
   Glory all around Him:
   Shepherds saw the wondrous sight,
   Heard the angels singing;
   All the plains were lit that night,
   All the hills were ringing.

3. Gentle Mary laid her Child
   Lowly in a manger;
   He is still the undefiled,
   But no more a stranger:
   Son of God, of humble birth,
   Beautiful the story;
   Praise His Name in all the earth,
   Hail the King of glory!

   Joseph Simpson Cook, 1859-1933

---

[3]Sing to "Tempus Adest Floridum," the tune used for "Good King Wenceslas."

Go, tell it on the mountain

1. While shepherds kept their watching
   O'er silent flocks by night,
   Behold throughout the heavens
   There shone a holy light

   Go, tell it on the mountain
   Over the hills and everywhere
   Go, tell it on the mountain
   That Jesus Christ is born.

2. The shepherds feared and trembled
   When lo! above the earth
   Rang out the angel chorus
   That hailed our Saviour's birth;

3. Down in a lowly manger
   The humble Christ was born;
   And God sent out salvation
   That blessed Christmas morn.

4. When I was a seeker
   I sought both night and day
   I sought the Lord to help me
   And He showed me the way.

5. He made me a watchman
   Upon the city wall
   And If I am a Christian
   I am the least of all.

John Wesley Work, Jr., 1907
from African-American Spiritual, early 1800s

God rest you merry, gentlemen

1. God rest you merry, gentlemen,
   Let nothing you dismay.
   For Jesus Christ our Savior,
   Was born on Christmas Day;
   To save us all from Satan's power,
   When we were gone astray.

   O tidings of comfort and joy,
   Comfort and joy;
   O tidings of comfort and joy.

2. In Bethlehem, in Jury,
   This blessed Babe was born,
   And laid within a manger,
   Upon this blessed morn;
   The which His mother Mary
   Did nothing take in scorn.

3. From God our heavenly Father,
   A blessed angel came.
   And unto certain shepherds,
   Brought tidings of the same,
   How that in Bethlehem was born,
   The Son of God by name:

4. Fear not, then said the Angel,
   Let nothing you affright,
   This day is born a Savior,
   Of virtue, power, and might;
   So frequently to vanquish all,
   The friends of Satan quite;

continued...

5   The shepherds at those tidings,
      Rejoiced much in mind,
      And left their flocks a feeding,
      In tempest, storm, and wind,
      And went to Bethlehem straightway,
      This blessed babe to find:

6   But when to Bethlehem they came,
      Whereas this infant lay
      They found him in a manger,
      Where oxen feed on hay;
      His mother Mary kneeling,
      Unto the Lord did pray:

7   With sudden joy and gladness
      The shepherds were beguiled,
      To see the Babe if Israel,
      Before His mother mild,
      O then with joy and cheerfulness
      Rejoice, each mother's child.

8   Now to the Lord sing praises,
      All you within this place,
      And with true love and brotherhood,
      Each other now embrace;
      This holy tide of Christmas,
      Doth bring redeeming grace.

9   God bless the ruler of this house,
      And send him long to reign,
      And many a merry Christmas
      May live to see again;
      Among your friends and kindred
      That live both far and near.

Trad. English, 18th Century

Good Christian men, rejoice

1. Good Christian men, rejoice
With heart, and soul, and voice;
Give ye heed to what we say:
News! News!
Jesus Christ was born to-day:
Ox and ass before Him bow,
And He is in the manger now.
Christ is born today! Christ is born today.

2. Good Christian men, rejoice,
With heart, and soul, and voice;
Now ye hear of endless bliss:
Joy! Joy!
Jesus Christ was born for this!
He hath openned heaven's door,
and man is blessed forevermore.
Christ was born for this! Christ was born for this!

3. Good Christian men, rejoice
With heart, and soul, and voice;
Now ye need not fear the grave:
Peace! Peace!
Jesus Christ was born to save!
Calls you one, and calls you all,
To gain His everlasting hall:
Christ was born to save! Christ was born to save!

Heinrich Suso, c. 1295-1366
Trans. John Mason Neale, 1818-1866

Good King Wenceslas

1. Good King Wenceslas look'd out,
On the Feast of Stephen;
When the snow lay round about,
Deep, and crisp, and even:
Brightly shone the moon that night,
Though the frost was cruel,
When a poor man came in sight,
Gath'ring winter fuel.

2. "Hither page and stand by me,
If thou know'st it, telling,
Yonder peasant, who is he?
Where and what his dwelling?"
"Sire, he lives a good league hence.
Underneath the mountain;
Right against the forest fence,
By Saint Agnes' fountain."

3. "Bring me flesh, and bring me wine,
Bring me pine-logs hither:
Thou and I will see him dine,
When we bear them thither."
Page and monarch forth they went,
Forth they went together;
Through the rude winds wild lament,
And the bitter weather.

4 "Sire, the night is darker now,
And the wind blows stronger;
Fails my heart, I know now how,
I can go no longer."
"Mark my footsteps, good my page;
Tread thou in them boldly;
Thou shalt find the winter's rage
Freeze thy blood less coldly."

5 In his master's steps he trod,
Where the snow lay dinted;
Heat was in the very sod
Which the saint had printed.
Therefore, Christian men, be sure,
Wealth or rank possessing,
Ye who now will bless the poor,
Shall yourselves find blessing.

John Mason Neale, 1818-1866

Hark! The Herald Angels sing

1. Hark! The Herald Angels sing,
"Glory to the new-born King;
Peace on earth, and mercy mild,
God and sinners reconciled!"
Joyful, all ye nations, rise.
Join the triumph of the skies.
With th' Angelic Hosts proclaim,
"Christ is born in Bethlehem!"
Hark! the herald angels sing,
"Glory to the new-born King."

2. Christ, by highest heaven adored,
Christ, the everlasting lord
Late in time behold Him come,
Off-spring of a Virgin's womb
Veiled in flesh the Godhead see,
Hail, the incarnate deity
Pleased as Man with men to dwell,
Jesus, our Emmanuel.
Hark! the herald angels sing,
"Glory to the New-born king!"

3. Hail the heav'n-born Prince of Peace,
Hail, the Sun of Righteousness
Light and life to all He brings,
Risen with healing in His Wings.
Mild He lays His Glory by,
Born that man no more may die
Born to raise the sons of earth,
Born to give them second birth.
Hark! the herald angels sing,
"Glory to the New-born king!"

4 Come, Desire of nations come,
  Fix in us Thy humble home;
  Oh, to all Thyself impart,
  Formed in each believing heart!
  Hark! the herald angels sing,
  "Glory to the new-born king;
  Peace on earth and mercy mild,
  God and sinners reconciled!"
  Hark! the herald angels sing,
  "Glory to the New-born king!"

5 Adam's likeness, Lord, efface,
  Stamp Thine image in its place:
  Second Adam from above,
  Reinstate us in Thy love.
  Let us Thee, though lost, regain,
  Thee, the Life, the inner man:
  O, to all Thyself impart,
  Formed in each believing heart.
  Hark! the herald angels sing,
  "Glory to the New-born king!"

Charles Wesley, 1707-1788, alt.

The holly and the ivy

1. The holly and the ivy,
   Now both are full well grown.
   Of all the trees that are in the wood,
   The holly bears the crown.

   Oh, the rising of the sun,
   The running of the deer.
   The playing of the merry organ,
   Sweet singing in the quire.

2. The holly bears a blossom
   As white as lily flower;
   And Mary bore sweet Jesus Christ
   To be our sweet Savior.

3. The holly bears a berry
   As red as any blood;
   And Mary bore sweet Jesus Christ
   To do poor sinners good.

4. The holly bears a prickle
   As sharp as any thorn;
   And Mary bore sweet Jesus Christ
   On Christmas day in the morn.

5. The holly bears a bark
   As bitter as any gall;
   And Mary bore sweet Jesus Christ
   For to redeem us all.

6. The holly and the ivy,
   When they are both full grown,
   Of all the trees that are in the wood,
   The holly bears the crown.

Trad. French

I wonder as I wander

1. I wonder as I wander out under the sky,
   How Jesus the Savior did come for to die.
   For poor on'ry people like you and like I...
   I wonder as I wander out under the sky.

2. When Mary birthed Jesus 'twas in a cow's stall,
   With wise men and farmers and shepherds and all.
   But high from God's heaven a star's light did fall,
   And the promise of ages it then did recall.

3. If Jesus had wanted for any wee thing,
   A star in the sky, or a bird on the wing,
   Or all of God's angels in heav'n for to sing,
   He surely could have it, 'cause he was the King.

Collected in NC by John Jacob Niles, 1933

In the bleak mid-winter

1. In the bleak mid-winter
Frosty wind made moan,
Earth stood hard as iron,
Water like a stone;
Snow had fallen, snow on snow,
Snow on snow,
In the bleak mid-winter
Long ago.

2. Our God, Heaven cannot hold Him
Nor earth sustain;
Heaven and earth shall flee away
When He comes to reign:
In the bleak mid-winter
A stable-place sufficed
The Lord God Almighty,
Jesus Christ.

3. Enough for Him, whom cherubim
Worship night and day,
A breastful of milk
And a mangerful of hay;
Enough for Him, whom angels
Fall down before,
The ox and ass and camel
Which adore.

4. Angels and archangels
May have gathered there,
Cherubim and seraphim
Thronged the air,

But only His mother
In her maiden bliss,
Worshipped the Beloved
With a kiss.

5 What can I give Him,
Poor as I am?
If I were a shepherd
I would bring a lamb,
If I were a wise man
I would do my part,
Yet what I can I give Him,
Give my heart.

Christina Georgina Rossetti, 1830-1894

Infant holy, Infant lowly

1 Infant holy, Infant lowly,
Lying cradled in a stall.
Oxes lowing little knowing
That the Babe is Lord of All.
Swift are winging Angels singing
Nowels ringing, Tidings bringing
That the Babe is Lord of All.

2 Flocks were sleeping, shepherds keeping
In the fields their vigil true.
Saw the glory, heard the story
Which should bless the world anew.
Christians kneeling and appealing
For the healing truth, revealing
That the Babe is born for you.

Trad. Polish
Trans. Edith Margaret Gellibrand Reed, 1885-1933

Infant holy, Infant lowly (alt. version)

1. Infant holy, Infant lowly,
   for His bed a cattle stall;
   Oxen lowing, little knowing,
   Christ the Babe is Lord of all.
   Swift are winging Angels singing,
   Noels ringing, Tidings bringing:
   Christ the Babe is Lord of all.

2. Flocks were sleeping, Shepherds keeping
   vigil till the morning new
   Saw the glory, heard the story,
   tidings of a gospel true.
   Thus rejoicing, free from sorrow,
   praises voicing, greet the morrow:
   Christ the Babe was born for you.

Trad. Polish
Trans. Edith Margaret Gellibrand Reed, 1885-1933

It came upon the midnight clear

1. It came upon the midnight clear,
   That glorious song of old,
   From angels bending near the earth,
   To touch their harps of gold;
   "Peace on the earth, good will to men,
   From heaven's all gracious King."
   The world in solemn stillness lay,
   To hear the angels sing.

2. Still through the cloven skies they come,
   With peaceful wings unfurl
   And still their heavenly music floats,
   O'er all the weary world.

Above its sad and lowly plains,
They bend on hovering wing
And ever o'er its Babel sounds,
The blessed angels sing.

3 Yet with the woes of sin and strife,
The world has suffered long;
Beneath the angel-strain have rolled,
Two thousand years of wrong;
And man, at war with man, hears not,
The love song which they bring:
O hush the noise, ye men of strife,
And hear the angels sing.

4 And ye, beneath life's crushing load,
Whose forms are bending low
Who toil along the climbing way
With painful steps and slow
Look now! for glad and golden hours
Come swiftly on the wing
O rest beside the weary road
And hear the angels sing.

5 For lo! the days are hastening on,
By prophet bards foretold,
When, with the ever-circling years,
Shall come the Age of Gold;7
When peace shall over all the earth,
Its ancient splendors fling,
And all the world give back the song,
Which now the angels sing.

Edmund Hamilton Sears, 1810-1876

Jesu, Bright And Morning Star

Jesu, bright and morning Star,
Uncreated Light of ages,
Star of Jacob, seen afar,
Guide our footsteps with yon Sages,
Till we also, of thy grace,
See thy face.
If the timid mariner
Do but eye thee, Star of morrow,
Though the winter night be drear,
Courage high he straight will borrow,
Soon will gain the port, where he
Fain would be.
Wonder-Star of eastern skies,
Grant that, at thy next appearing,
With our bodies we may rise,
Joyfully thy summons hearing,
And to realms of endless clay
Wend our way.

Anon.

Joy to the world

1 Joy to the world! The Lord is come:
Let earth receive her King,
Let every heart prepare him room,
And heaven and nature sing.

2 Joy to the earth! The Saviour reigns:
Let men their songs employ;
While fields and floods, rocks, hills and plains
Repeat the sounding joy.

3 No more let sin and sorrow grow,
Nor thorns infest the ground:
He comes to make His blessings flow
Far as the curse is found.

4 He rules the world with truth and grace,
And makes the nations prove
The glories of his righteousness
And wonders of his love.

Isaac Watts, 1674-1748

Judge eternal, throned in splendor

1 Judge eternal, throned in splendor,
Lord of lords and King of kings,
With Thy living fire of judgment
Purge this land of bitter things;
Solace all its wide dominion
With the healing of thy wings.

2 Still the weary folk are pining
For the hour that brings release,
And the city's crowded clangor
Cries aloud for sin to cease;
And the homesteads and the woodlands
Plead in silence for their peace.

3 Crown, O God, thine own endeavor;
Cleave our darkness with Thy sword;
Feed the faint and hungry heathen
With the richness of Thy word;
Cleanse the body of this nation
Through the glory of the Lord.

Henry Scott Holland, 1902, 1909

Lo, how a rose e'er blooming

1. Lo, how a rose e'er blooming,
   From tender stem hath sprung!
   From Jesse's lineage coming,
   As men of old have sung.
   It came, a floweret bright,
   Amid the cold of winter
   When half spent was the night

2. Isaiah 'twas foretold it,
   The Rose I have in mind
   With Mary we behold it,
   The Virgin mother kind
   To show God's love aright,
   She bore to us a Savior
   When half spent was the night

3. The shepherds heard the story
   Proclaimed by angels bright,
   How Christ, the Lord of Glory
   Was born on earth this night.
   To Bethlehem they sped
   And in the manger they found him,
   As angels heralds said.

4. This Flower, whose fragrance tender
   With sweetness fills the air,
   Dispels with glorious splendor
   The darkness everywhere;
   True man, yet very God,
   From Sin and death he saves us,
   And lightens every load.

> 15th C. German carol, Trans. Theodore Baker, 1894 (vv. 1-2)
> Friedrich Layritz, 1808-59; Trans. Harried R. Kraugh (vv. 3-4)

Mortals, awake, the morning is breaking

1. Mortals, awake, the morning is breaking,
Christians, rejoice, for the day is at hand;
See in the manger the Infant adoring,
Shepherds and Angels, a wondering band.
Who is the tender Babe gently reposing
Mid cattle and strangers in yon humble stall?
Tis Christ the Anointed, who, from the beginning,
Is Sov'reign, Creator, and Lord over all.

Hail the Incarnate One, Holy and Glorious,
Saviour, Emmanuel, God with us.

2. Shepherds, arise, reveal the strange story
How through the darkness there shone all around
Light far exceeding the sun in its glory;
Trembling ye gaz'd as ye lay on the ground;
How there appeared an Angel declaring
The message of mercy: "Glad tidings I bring,"
Salvation on high for mankind preparing,
Earth has received a Heavenly King.

3. Morals fall down in devout adoration,
Christians unite in the heavenly strains;
Join in the chorus of loud exultation
Carol'd by Angels on Palestine's plains,
Let the still air ring with music sublimest,
And echo in praises creation to fill;
All honour and glory to God in the Highest,
Peace be on Earth, unto all men good will.

Anon.

Noel, Noel, Noel

1. Noel, Noel, Noel,
   Now together sing!
   Faithful people crying.
   'Lord, our thanks we bring'
   Singing Noel, Noel, To Him our little King,
   Noel, Noel, Noel
   Let your voices ring.

2. Clearly spake the Angel:
   'Shepherds, come away!
   Peaceful and rejoicing
   Bethlem seek this day!
   This little Lamb is born to be our King!'
   Noel, Noel, Noel
   Let your voices ring.

3. There they found together
   Joseph – Mary blest –
   Cradling from the weather
   Jesus at Her breast
   Only a manger for the Heavenly King!
   Noel, Noel, Noel
   Let your voices ring.

4. Kings draw nigh to greet Him,
   Neath the shining star,
   Seeking Bethlem city
   From their countries far.
   Here, in the dawn they find their Infant King!
   Noel, Noel, Noel
   Let your voices ring.

5   See! One beareth incense,
Others, gold and myrrh!
Offering them to Jesus
Sleeping sweetly there.
See! In the manger, beauty blossoming!
Noel, Noel, Noel
Let your voices ring.

6   See our Saviour Jesus
Who, by His great deeds
From despair will save us,
Dying for our needs.
Shedding His blood, that all the world may sing,
Noel, Noel, Noel
Let your voices ring.

Trad. French
Trans. K. W. Simpson, c. 1930

O come, all ye faithful

1. O come, all ye faithful, Joyful and triumphant,
O Come ye, O come ye, to Bethlehem.
Come and behold Him, Born the King of angels;

O come, let us adore Him,
O come, let us adore Him,
O come, let us adore Him,
Christ the Lord.

2. God of God, Light of Light,
Lo! he abhors not the Virgin's womb;
Very God, Begotten not created.

3. Sing, choirs of angels, Sing in exultation;
Sing, all ye citizens of heaven above!
Glory to God, In the highest;

4. Yea, Lord, we greet Thee, Born this happy morning;
Jesu, to Thee be glory given;
Word of the Father, Now in flesh appearing.

John Francis Wade c. 1711-1786
Trans. Frederick Oakeley, 1802-1880

O come, O come, Emmanuel

1. O come, O come, Emmanuel,
   And ransom captive Israel,
   That mourns in lonely exile here
   Until the Son of God appear.

   Rejoice! Rejoice! Emmanuel
   Shall come to thee, O Israel.

2. O come, Thou Rod of Jesse, free
   Thine own from Satan's tyranny;
   From depths of hell Thy people save,
   And give them victory o'er the grave.

3. O come, Thou Day-Spring, come and cheer
   Our spirits by Thine advent here;
   Disperse the gloomy clouds of night
   And death's dark shadows put to flight!

4. O come, Thou Key of David, come,
   And open wide our heavenly home;
   Make safe the way that leads on high,
   And close the path to misery.

5. O come, O come, Thou Lord of Might,
   Who to Thy tribes on Sinai's height
   In ancient times didst give the law
   In cloud, and majesty, and awe.

8th Century Latin
Trans. John Mason Neale, alt.

O holy night

1. O holy night, the stars are brightly shining,
It is the night of the dear Savior's birth;
Long lay the world in sin and error pining,
Till He appeared and the soul felt its worth.
A thrill of hope the weary world rejoices,
For yonder breaks a new and glorious morn;

    Fall on your knees, Oh hear the angel voices!
    O night divine, O night when Christ was born!
    O night, O holy night, O night divine.

2. Led by the light of faith serenely beaming
With glowing hearts by His cradle we stand
So led by light of a star sweetly gleaming
Here come the wise men from Orient land
The King of Kings lay thus in lowly manger
In all our trials born to be our friend.

    He knows our need, He guardeth us from danger
    Behold your King! Before Him lowly bend!
    Behold your King! Before Him lowly bend!

3. Truly He taught us to love one another
His law is love and His gospel is peace
Chains shall He break, for the slave is our brother,
And in His name all oppression shall cease.
Sweet hymns of joy in grateful chorus raise we,
Let all within us praise His holy name.

    Christ is the Lord, O praise His name forever!
    His pow'r and glory evermore proclaim!
    His pow'r and glory evermore proclaim!

                                Placide Cappeau, 1808-1877
                          Trans. John Sullivan Dwight, 1813-1893

O little town of Bethlehem

1. O little town of Bethlehem,
   How still we see thee lie!
   Above thy deep and dreamless sleep
   The silent stars go by.
   Yet in thy dark streets shineth
   The everlasting Light;
   The hopes and fears of all the years
   Are met in thee to-night.

2. O morning stars, together
   Proclaim the holy birth!
   And praises sing to God the King,
   And peace to men on earth.
   For Christ is born of Mary
   And gathered all above,
   While mortals sleep the Angels keep
   Their watch of wondering love.

3. How silently, how silently,
   The wondrous gift is given;
   So God imparts to human hearts
   The blessings of His Heaven.
   No ear may hear His coming,
   But in this world of sin,
   Where meek souls will receive Him still,
   The dear Christ enters in.

continued...

4 O holy Child of Bethlehem,
    Descend to us, we pray!
    Cast out our sin and enter in,
    Be born in us to-day.
    We hear the Christmas angels,
    The great glad tidings tell;
    O come to us, abide with us,
    Our Lord Emmanuel!

Bishop Phillips Brooks, 1835-1893

Of the Father's love begotten

1 Of the Father's love begotten,
    Ere the worlds began to be,
    He is Alpha and Omega,
    He the source, the ending He,
    Of the things that are, that have been,
    And that future years shall see,
    Evermore and evermore!

2 At His Word the worlds were framèd;
    He commanded; it was done:
    Heaven and earth and depths of ocean
    In their threefold order one;
    All that grows beneath the shining
    Of the moon and burning sun,
    Evermore and evermore!

3 He is found in human fashion,
    Death and sorrow here to know,
    That the race of Adam's children
    Doomed by law to endless woe,
    May not henceforth die and perish
    In the dreadful gulf below,
    Evermore and evermore!

4. O that birth forever blessèd,
   When the Virgin, full of grace,
   By the Holy Ghost conceiving,
   Bare the Savior of our race;
   And the Babe, the world's Redeemer,
   First revealed His sacred face,
   Evermore and evermore!

5. This is He Whom seers in old time
   Chanted of with one accord;
   Whom the voices of the prophets
   Promised in their faithful word;
   Now He shines, the long expected,
   Let creation praise its Lord,
   Evermore and evermore!

6. O ye heights of heaven adore Him;
   Angel hosts, His praises sing;
   Powers, dominions, bow before Him,
   And extol our God and King!
   Let no tongue on earth be silent,
   Every voice in concert sing,
   Evermore and evermore!

7. Righteous judge of souls departed,
   Righteous King of them that live,
   On the Father's throne exalted
   None in might with Thee may strive;
   Who at last in vengeance coming
   Sinners from Thy face shalt drive,
   Evermore and evermore!

continued...

8 Thee let old men, thee let young men,
Thee let boys in chorus sing;
Matrons, virgins, little maidens,
With glad voices answering:
Let their guileless songs re-echo,
And the heart its music bring,
Evermore and evermore!

9 Christ, to Thee with God the Father,
And, O Holy Ghost, to Thee,
Hymn and chant with high thanksgiving,
And unwearied praises be:
Honor, glory, and dominion,
And eternal victory,
Evermore and evermore!

Aurelius Clemens Prudentius, 348-405
Trans. John Mason Neale, 1818-1866 &
Henry Williams Baker, 1821-1877

Once in royal David's city

1 Once in royal David's city
Stood a lowly cattle shed,
Where a mother laid her Baby
In a manger for His bed:
Mary was that mother mild,
Jesus Christ her little Child.

2 He came down to earth from heaven,
Who is God and Lord of all,
And His shelter was a stable,
And His cradle was a stall;
With the poor, and mean, and lowly,
Lived on earth our Savior holy.

3. And through all His wondrous childhood
   He would honor and obey,
   Love and watch the lowly maiden,
   In whose gentle arms He lay:
   Christian children all must be
   Mild, obedient, good as He.

4. For he is our childhood's pattern;
   Day by day, like us He grew;
   He was little, weak and helpless,
   Tears and smiles like us He knew;
   And He feeleth for our sadness,
   And He shareth in our gladness.

5. And our eyes at last shall see Him,
   Through His own redeeming love;
   For that Child so dear and gentle
   Is our Lord in heaven above,
   And He leads His children on
   To the place where He is gone.

6. Not in that poor lowly stable,
   With the oxen standing by,
   We shall see Him; but in heaven,
   Set at God's right hand on high;
   Where like stars His children crowned
   All in white shall wait around.

Cecil Frances Humphreys Alexander, 1848

Silent night! Holy night!

1. Silent night! Holy night!
   All is calm, all is bright,
   Round yon Virgin Mother and Child!
   Holy Infant, so tender and mild,
   Sleep in heavenly peace!
   Sleep in heavenly peace!

2. Silent night! Holy night!
   Shepherds quake at the sight!3
   Glories stream from Heaven afar,
   Heavenly Hosts sing Alleluia!
   Christ, the Saviour, is born!
   Christ, the Saviour, is born!

3. Silent night! Holy night!
   Son of God, love's pure light
   Radiant beams from Thy Holy Face
   With the dawn of redeeming grace,
   Jesus, Lord, at Thy Birth!
   Jesus, Lord, at Thy Birth!

4. Silent night, Holy night,
   Wondrous star, lend thy light
   With the angels let us sing
   Alleluia to our King
   Christ the Savior is here,
   Jesus the Savior is here!

Rev. Joseph Mohr, 1816 (vv. 1-3)
Trans. Bishop John Freeman Young, 1820-1885
v. 4 Anon.

Sing we now of Christmas

1. Sing we now of Christmas,
   Noel sing we here.
   Sing our grateful praises
   To the maid so dear.

   Sing we Noel!
   The King is born, Noel!
   Sing we now of Christmas.
   Sing we here, Noel!

2. From the Eastern kingdoms
   Come the wise men far.
   Bearing ancient treasure,
   Following yonder star.

3. From the distant mountains,
   Hear the trumpet sound.
   With angelic blessings
   On the silent town.

4. Come let us surround Him
   On this magic night.
   Gather here around Him,
   Wondrous Babe of light.

Trad. French and English

Still, still, still

1. Still, still, still.
   The night is cold and chill!
   The virgin's tender arms enfolding,
   Warm and safe the Christ child holding.
   Still, still, still,
   The night is cold and chill.

2. Still, still, still
   One can hear the falling snow.
   For all is hushed, the world is sleeping,
   Holy Star its vigil keeping.
   Still, still, still,
   One can hear the falling snow.

3. Sleep, sleep, sleep,
   'Tis the eve of our Saviour's birth.
   The night is peaceful all around you,
   Close your eyes, let sleep surround you.
   Sleep, sleep, sleep
   'Tis the eve of our Saviour's birth.

4. Dream, dream, dream,
   Of the joyous day to come.
   While guardian angels without number
   Watch you as you sweetly slumber.
   Dream, dream, dream,
   Of the joyous day to come

Trad. Austrian

The Wassail Song

1. Here we come a-caroling
   Among the leaves so green,
   Here we come a wand'ring,
   So fair to be seen.

   Love and joy come to you,
   And to your carol too
   And God bless you and send you a Happy New Year,
   And God send you a Happy New Year.

2. We are not daily beggars
   Who beg from door to door,
   But we are neighbors' children,
   Whom you have seen before.

3. God bless the Master of this house,
   Likewise the Mistress too
   And all the little children,
   That round the table go.

4. And all your kin and kinfolk
   That dwell both far and near
   We wish a Merry Christmas
   And Happy New Year.

   Trad. English (adaptation)

We three kings of Orient are

3 KINGS:

1. We three kings of Orient are
   Bearing gifts, we traverse afar.
   Field and fountain, moor and mountain,
   Following yonder star.

   O Star of Wonder, Star of Night,
   Star with Royal Beauty bright,
   Westward leading, Still proceeding,
   Guide us to Thy perfect Light.

GASPAR:

2. Born a King on Bethlehem plain,
   Gold I bring to crown Him again,
   King forever,
   Ceasing never
   Over us all to reign.

MELCHIOR:

3. Frankincense to offer have I;
   Incense owns a Deity nigh:
   Prayer and praising
   All men raising,
   Worship Him God on high.

BALTHAZAR:

4. Myrrh is mine; it's bitter perfume;
   Breathes a life of gathering gloom: —
   Sorrowing, sighing,
   Bleeding, dying,
   Sealed in the stone-cold tomb.

3 KINGS:
5 Glorious now behold Him arise,
King and God and sacrifice.
Heav'n sings
Halleluia;
Hallelujah the earth replies.

John Henry Hopkins, Jr., 1820-1891

Wexford Carol

1 Good people all, this Christmas-time,
Consider well and bear in mind
What our good God for us has done
In sending his beloved Son.
With Mary holy we should pray
To God with love this Christmas day;
In Bethlehem upon that morn
There was a blessed Messiah born.

2 The night before that happy tide
The noble Virgin and her guide
Were long time seeking up and down
To find a lodging in the town.
But mark how all things came to pass;
From every door repelled alas!
As long foretold, their refuge all
Was but an humble ox's stall.

continued...

3   There were three wise men from afar
Directed by a glorious star,
And on they wandered night and day
Until they came where Jesus lay,
And when they came unto that place
Where our beloved Messiah was,
They humbly cast them at his feet,
With gifts of gold and incense sweet.

4   Near Bethlehem did shepherds keep
Their flocks of lambs and feeding sheep;
To whom God's angels did appear,
Which put the shepherds in great fear.
'Prepare and go.' the angels said.
'To Bethlehem, be not afraid;
For there you'll find, this happy morn,
A princely babe, sweet Jesus born.'

5   With thankful heart and joyful mind,
The shepherds went the babe to find,
And as God's angel had foretold,
They did our saviour Christ behold.
Within a manger he was laid,
And by his side the virgin maid,
Attending on the Lord of life,
Who came on earth to end all strife.

Anon.

What Child is this?

1. What Child is this who, laid to rest
   On Mary's lap is sleeping?
   Whom Angels greet with anthems sweet,
   While shepherds watch are keeping?

2. This, this is Christ the King,
   Whom shepherds guard and Angels sing;
   Haste, haste, to bring Him laud,
   The Babe, the Son of Mary.

3. Why lies He in such mean estate,
   Where ox and ass are feeding?
   Good Christians, fear, for sinners here
   The silent Word is pleading.

4. Nails, spear shall pierce Him through,
   The cross be borne for me, for you.
   Hail, hail the Word made flesh,
   The Babe, the Son of Mary.

5. So bring Him incense, gold and myrrh,
   Come peasant, king to own Him;
   The King of kings salvation brings,
   Let loving hearts enthrone Him.

6. Raise, raise a song on high,
   The virgin sings her lullaby.
   Joy, joy for Christ is born,
   The Babe, the Son of Mary.

William Chatterton Dix, 1837-1865

While shepherds watched

1. Whilst Shepherds watched their flocks by night,
   All seated on the ground,
   The Angel of the Lord came down,
   And glory shone all around.

2. "Fear not, said he, for mighty dread
   Had seized their troubled mind,
   Glad tidings of great joy I bring
   To you and all mankind.

3. To you in David's town this day
   Is born of David's line
   A Saviour, which is Christ the Lord,
   And this shall be the sign.

4. The heav'nly Babe you there shall find,
   To human view display'd,
   All meanly wrapp't in swaddling bands,
   And in a manger laid.

5. Thus spake the Seraph, and forthwith
   Appeared a shining throng
   Of Angels, praising God, and thus
   Addressed their joyful song:

6. "All glory be to God on high,
   And to the earth be peace;
   Good-will henceforth from Heaven to men
   Begin and never cease."

Nahum Tate, 1700
this vers. from Davies Gilbert, 1822

Zacharias being an aged man

1. Zacharias being an aged man,
Well stricken on in years,
The Angel Gabriel to him came,
And unto him appears,
And told him what the Lord had said:
In those his latter days
His barren wife should bear a son,
Which should his glory raise.

Nowel, Nowel, Nowel, Nowel,
Nowel, Nowel, Nowel,
We may rejoice to hear the voice
Of the Angel Gabriel.

2. What sign, said he, wilt thou shew me,
That I should have a son?
The Angel said, till he be born,
Thou shalt be stricken dumb.
And presently his speech was gone,
A word he could not say;
Because of his great unbelief,
The same was taken away.

3. But when his wife was big with child,
Her cousin Mary came,
To visit her in friendly sort,
When she did hear the same:
And when she came before her sight,
Bearing our Heavenly King,
The tender Infant in her womb,
For very joy did spring.

continued...

4 But when the time of birth was come,
    She was deliver'd then,
    And, as the Angel did command,
    His name was called John;
    He did baptise both old and young,
    That did before him stand;
    And still he cried, Repent, Repent,
    God's judgments are at hand.

5 His cloathing was of camels' hair;
    Wild honey was his meat;
    His dwelling was in wilderness,
    As Scripture doth repeat;
    Till that in prison at the last
    He ended his mortal life,
    Because he did reprove the King,
    That took his brother's wife.

Trad. English

Index of Hymns & Carols

All my heart this night rejoices 4
Angels from the realms of glory 6
Angels we have heard on high 7
As it fell out upon a day 16
As with gladness, men of old 8
Away in a manger 9
The Birthday of a King 9
Break forth, O beauteous heavenly light 10
Bring a torch, Jeanette, Isabella 11
Carol of the bells 12
Child in the manger 12
Come, Thou long-expected Jesus 13
Deck the hall 14
Ding Dong! merrily on high 15
Dives and Lazarus 16
The first Nowell 18
Fum, Fum, Fum 20
Gentle Mary laid her Child 21
Go, tell it on the mountain 22
God rest you merry, gentlemen 23
Good Christian men, rejoice 25
Good King Wenceslas 26
Good people all, this Christmas-time 55
Hark! How the bells 12
Hark! The Herald Angels sing 28
Here we come a-caroling 53

The holly and the ivy 30
I wonder as I wander 31
In the bleak mid-winter 32
In the little village of Bethlehem 9
Infant holy, Infant lowly 33
It came upon the midnight clear 34
Jesu, Bright And Morning Star 36
Joy to the world 36
Judge eternal, throned in splendor 37
Lo, how a rose e'er blooming 38
Mortals, awake, the morning is breaking 39
Noel, Noel, Noel 40
O come, all ye faithful 42
O come, O come, Emmanuel 43
O little town of Bethlehem 45
Of the Father's love begotten 46
On this joyful Christmas Day 20
Once in royal David's city 48
Silent night! Holy night! 50
Sing we now of Christmas 51
Still, still, still 52
The Wassail Song..53
We three kings of Orient are 54
Wexford Carol 55
What Child is this? 57
While shepherds kept their watching 22
While shepherds watched 58
Zacharias being an aged man 59

Colophon

This book was typeset using the Memoir package in LaTeX.

The font is Minion Pro, designed by Robert Slimbach. Body text is set at an 11 point weight.

www.ingramcontent.com/pod-product-compliance
Lightning Source LLC
Chambersburg PA
CBHW071411040426
42444CB00009B/2197